Lerner SPORTS

SUPER SPORTS TEAMS

INSIDE THE CHICAGO BEARS

CHRISTINA HILL

Lerner Publications ◆ Minneapolis

SPORTS THRILLS *MEET* RESEARCH SKILLS

Lerner SPORTS

Free Database Trial: **lernersports.com**

Lerner Publications Company
An imprint of Lerner Publishing Group, Inc.
241 First Avenue North
Minneapolis, MN 55401 USA

For reading levels and more information, look up this title at www.lernerbooks.com.

Main body text set in Aptifer Slab LT Pro / Typeface provided by Linotype AG

Library of Congress Cataloging-in-Publication Data

Names: Hill, Christina, author.
Title: Inside the Chicago Bears / Christina Hill.
Description: Minneapolis, MN : Lerner Publications, [2023] | Series: Super Sports Teams (Lerner Sports) | Includes bibliographical references and index. | Audience: Ages 7–11 years | Audience: Grades 2–3 | Summary: "The 1985 Chicago Bears might be the best team in NFL history. Explore the franchise's origins, why the '85 Bears were special, and which superstar players will carry Chicago to their next Super Bowl victory"— Provided by publisher.
Identifiers: LCCN 2021062948 (print) | LCCN 2021062949 (ebook) | ISBN 9781728458120 (Library Binding) | ISBN 9781728463391 (Paperback) | ISBN 9781728462349 (eBook)
Subjects: LCSH: Chicago Bears (Football team)—History—Juvenile literature. | Football players—Illinois— Chicago—History—Juvenile literature. | Football—Illinois—Chicago—History—Juvenile literature.
Classification: LCC GV956.C5 H55 2023 (print) | LCC GV956.C5 (ebook) | DDC 793.332/640977311—dc23/eng/20220114

LC record available at https://lccn.loc.gov/2021062948
LC ebook record available at https://lccn.loc.gov/2021062949

Manufactured in the United States of America
1 – CG – 7/15/22

TABLE OF CONTENTS

William "The Refrigerator" Perry (*center*) and teammates celebrate a Chicago Bears touchdown in the 1986 Super Bowl.

THE SURPRISE TOUCHDOWN

FACTS AT A GLANCE

- The **CHICAGO BEARS** played their first season in 1920 and are one of the oldest franchises in the National Football League (NFL).

- The Bears won the **SUPER BOWL** in 1986.

- **SOLDIER FIELD** is the oldest stadium in the NFL. It has been the home of the Bears since 1971.

- The Bears are often called the **MONSTERS OF THE MIDWAY**.

- Running back **WALTER PAYTON** is one of the greatest NFL players of all time.

On January 26, 1986, the Chicago Bears played in their first NFL Super Bowl. They faced the New England Patriots. The Patriots were also playing in their first Super Bowl.

Less than two minutes into the first quarter, the Patriots recovered a fumble. Then they kicked a 36-yard field goal. The score was one of the quickest in Super Bowl history.

The Bears struck back. Coached by former star player Mike Ditka, the Bears dominated after the opening minutes of the game. By halftime, they led 23–3. The Bears were known for their strong defense, which caused six Patriots turnovers. They held the Patriots to only seven rushing yards for the entire game.

One of the game's most memorable moments came during the third quarter. Bears quarterback Jim McMahon threw a 27-yard pass to wide receiver Dennis Gentry. The play brought the ball to New England's 1-yard line. On the next play, defensive player William Perry came onto the field. To everyone's surprise, McMahon handed the ball to Perry. Nicknamed The Refrigerator for his huge size, Perry plowed through the defense with ease. He spiked the ball in the end zone after scoring a touchdown.

The Bears won their first Super Bowl 46–10. Many football fans consider this Bears team to be one of the greatest NFL teams ever. Their strong offense and defense were simply the best. The Bears have been playing tough football for more than 100 years.

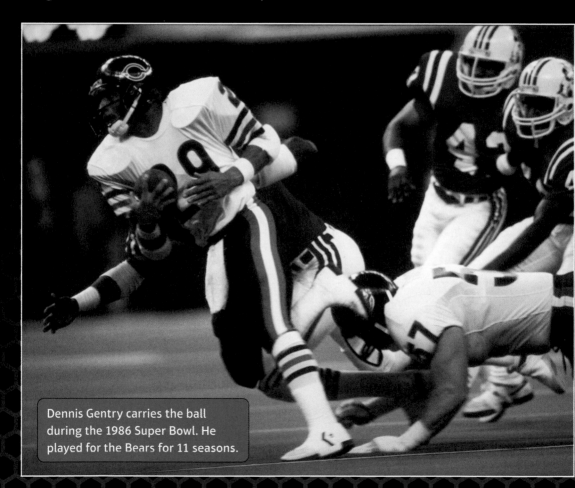

Dennis Gentry carries the ball during the 1986 Super Bowl. He played for the Bears for 11 seasons.

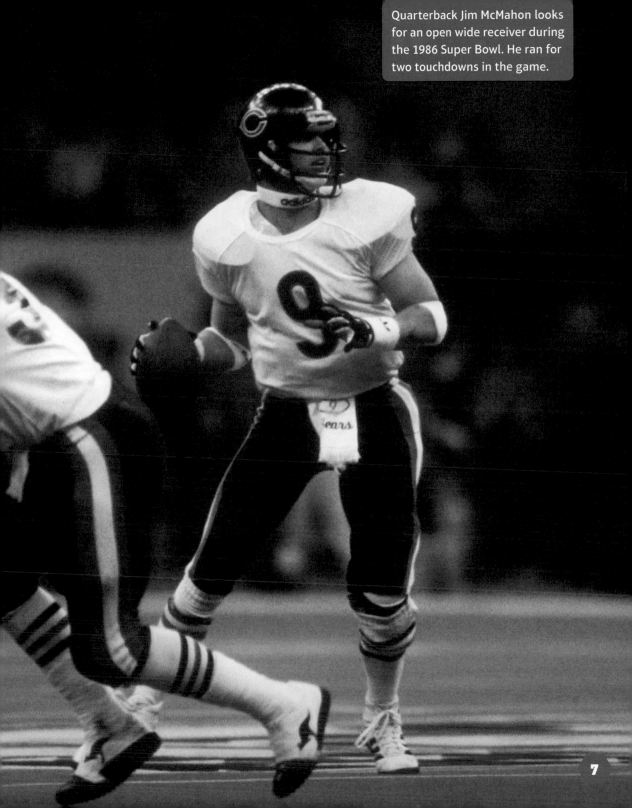

Quarterback Jim McMahon looks for an open wide receiver during the 1986 Super Bowl. He ran for two touchdowns in the game.

George Halas coached the Bears for 40 seasons.

MONSTERS OF THE MIDWAY

In 1920, businessperson A. E. Staley started the Chicago Bears franchise. The Bears are one of the oldest teams in the NFL. They started in Decatur, Illinois, and were called the Decatur Staleys. In 1921, the team moved to Chicago, Illinois. George Halas took over as the owner. Known as Papa Bear, Halas served as player, owner, and coach for the team. Halas ranks number two in NFL history with 318 coaching victories.

Members of the 1920 Decatur Staleys

In 1922, Halas changed the team name to the Bears. He wanted to honor the Chicago Cubs pro baseball team. Cubs are young bears. Halas also wanted people to think that football players are bigger than baseball players.

Virginia Halas McCaskey is one of four women who own an NFL franchise.

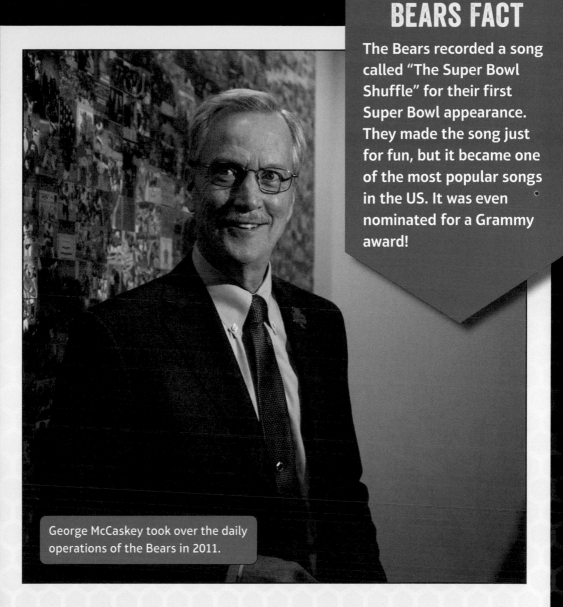

George McCaskey took over the daily operations of the Bears in 2011.

Halas coached the team until 1967 but continued to run the franchise until his death in 1983. His daughter Virginia has owned the team ever since. Her son George McCaskey manages and oversees the franchise.

Fans refer to their team as Da Bears and the Monsters of the Midway. The Midway is a 1-mile (1.6 km) strip of park in Chicago.

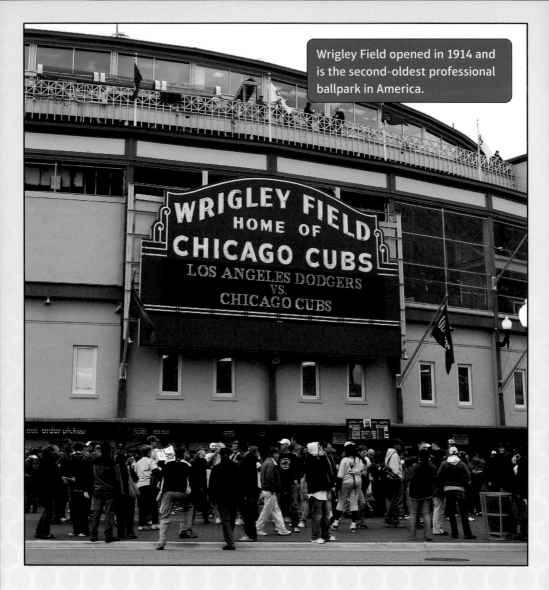

Wrigley Field opened in 1914 and is the second-oldest professional ballpark in America.

The Bears played their first 49 seasons in Chicago at Wrigley Field, home of the Cubs. In 1971, the Bears moved into Soldier Field in downtown Chicago. It has been their home stadium ever since and is the oldest stadium in the NFL. It was improved in 2003. Even after the big construction project, Soldier Field is still the smallest NFL stadium with 61,500 seats.

Soldier Field has hosted events since 1924. The stadium's name honors soldiers who died during World War I (1914–1918).

Running back Thomas Jones runs with the ball during the 2007 Super Bowl. The Indianapolis Colts won the game to give the Bears their only Super Bowl loss.

AMAZING MOMENTS

The Chicago Bears have a history of greatness on the football field. They have won one Super Bowl and eight NFL Championships. Their long team history is full of amazing moments.

In 1940, the Bears met Washington for the NFL Championship. Less than one minute into the game, the Bears proved that they were ready to win. Bears running back Bill Osmanski ran 68 yards and scored a touchdown. By halftime, the score was 28–0.

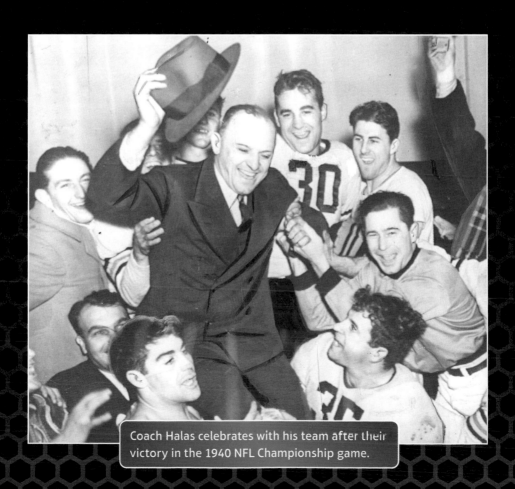

Coach Halas celebrates with his team after their victory in the 1940 NFL Championship game.

Despite their huge lead, the Bears never let up. Officials asked Halas to stop letting his team kick extra points after touchdowns. The officials were running out of footballs. There were no nets behind the goalposts, so kicked balls sailed into the hands of fans. The Bears crushed Washington 73–0. It remains the most one-sided victory in NFL history.

In 1963, the Bears faced the New York Giants for the NFL Championship title. The teams played at Wrigley Field in Chicago. The temperature was a freezing 9°F (–13°C). Both teams kept the score close throughout. They were tied at the end of the first quarter. The Giants took the lead in the second quarter with a score of 10–7. But the Bears came through at the end of the game with a final 1-yard touchdown. It gave them a 14–10 win.

George McAfee played for the Bears from 1940 to 1941 and 1945 to 1950. He helped lead the team to victory in the 1940 NFL Championship.

The Bears had only four winning seasons in the next 20 years. But in the 1980s, running back Walter Payton, quarterback Jim McMahon, and coach Mike Ditka joined the team. In 1985, they had a record 15 wins and one loss. The season ended with their big Super Bowl victory against the New England Patriots.

The Bears dominated the NFL's first six seasons with 34 shutout wins. A shutout happens when the opposing team doesn't score any points.

It took 21 years, but in 2007, the Bears had another chance at the Super Bowl. They faced the Indianapolis Colts. Rookie wide receiver Devin Hester received the opening kickoff for Chicago. He ran 92 yards for a touchdown. The Bears held the lead until the end of the second quarter. But they lost the game 29–17. Bears running back Thomas Jones rushed for 112 yards and caught four passes for 18 yards. Despite the loss, fans were thrilled to see Da Bears at another Super Bowl.

Devin Hester had 14 career punt return touchdowns and five kickoff return touchdowns.

Mike Ditka played for the Bears from 1961 to 1966, and he coached the team from 1982 to 1992.

BEARS SUPERSTARS

The Chicago Bears have had an endless roster of superstar players and coaches throughout the years. One of the earliest was halfback Red Grange, nicknamed the Galloping Ghost. He got his nickname for his unique running style. He shifted quickly back and forth as he ran, moving like a ghost would.

Red Grange was also called the Wheaton Ice Man because he sold ice in his hometown of Wheaton, Illinois, to earn money before his pro football career.

Grange was a popular college football player at the University of Illinois. Halas signed him for the Bears in 1925. Halas hoped that Grange would help boost the popularity of the new NFL, which began in 1920. His plan worked! Grange drew a crowd of 36,000 fans at his first NFL game.

The Bears drafted Sid Luckman in 1939. Halas wanted him to play quarterback, but Luckman lacked confidence. He fumbled the ball often and was unsure of his quarterback skills. Halas had faith in him and encouraged Luckman to keep practicing the position. Luckman's practice paid off. He led the Bears to four NFL Championships. He earned the Most Valuable Player (MVP) award for his quarterback skills in the 1943 season.

Sid Luckman tops the NFL charts with seven touchdown passes in a single game.

BEARS FACT

The Chicago Bears hold the NFL record with 34 players in the Pro Football Hall of Fame.

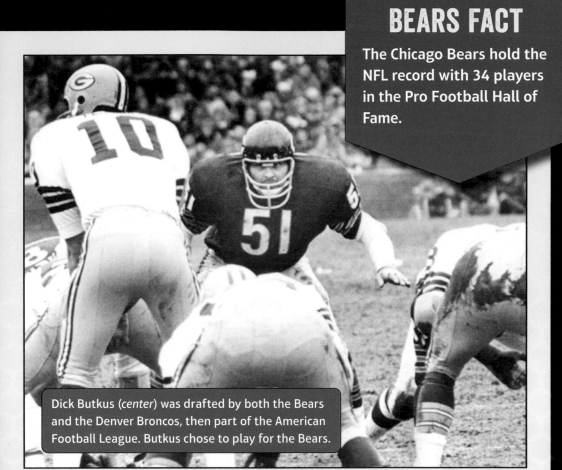

Dick Butkus (*center*) was drafted by both the Bears and the Denver Broncos, then part of the American Football League. Butkus chose to play for the Bears.

Even though he was an amazing player, Mike Ditka is best known as Coach Ditka. In 1961, his first season as a tight end for the Bears, Ditka had 12 touchdown catches and won NFL Rookie of the Year. He spent six seasons with the Bears before leaving to play for the Philadelphia Eagles. But Ditka returned to the Bears in 1982 and served as head coach for 11 seasons.

Linebacker Dick Butkus began his career with the Bears in 1965. He played nine seasons with the team. Butkus was selected to eight Pro Bowls. He was tough and strong on the field. The Bears retired his number 51 jersey to honor him and remember his time on the team. No Bears player has worn his number since.

Walter Payton runs with the ball. Each year, the Walter Payton NFL Man of the Year Award honors a player who excelled on the field and helped the community.

In 1975, one of the greatest NFL running backs of all time joined the Bears. Walter Payton, also known as Sweetness, played with the team until 1987. Payton ran for more than 1,000 yards ten times in his career. He was part of nine Pro Bowls, holds many franchise records, and won the NFL MVP award in 1977. He missed only one game in 13 seasons.

Linebacker Khalil Mack joined the Bears in 2018 after playing four seasons with the Oakland Raiders. Mack was great from the start. In his first game with the Bears, he had a sack, a forced fumble, a fumble recovery, an interception, and a touchdown. Mack has been a Pro Bowler six times in his NFL career.

Khalil Mack was the NFL Defensive Player of the Year in 2016.

Staley Da Bear is the team's official mascot. His name honors the team's first owner, A. E. Staley.

BEAR DOWN!

The Bears are one of the oldest teams in NFL history, keeping their fans cheering in the stands since 1920. Every time the Bears score a touchdown during a home game, stadium speakers play a special song called "Bear Down, Chicago Bears." Fans chant "bear down" as they cheer on their team.

After playing more than 50 years at Soldier Field, it was time for a big move. In 2021, the Bears started making plans to build a new stadium in Arlington Heights, Illinois. Construction will take around two years to finish. Fans are excited to fill the new stands with their team colors of orange, navy, and white.

Bears fans are always excited to cheer for their favorite players.

The 2021 Bears roster included rookie Justin Fields. The former college superstar could be Chicago's next great quarterback. The team's promising lineup includes players such as Khalil Mack, Germain Ifedi, and Mario Edwards Jr. With new head coach Matt Eberflus and a brand-new stadium coming soon, Bears fans are ready for the Monsters of the Midway to have many winning seasons ahead.

Quarterback Justin Fields was the 11th overall pick in the 2021 NFL Draft.

After four seasons with the Seattle Seahawks, offensive tackle Germain Ifedi joined the Bears in 2020.

BEARS
SEASON RECORD
HOLDERS

RUSHING TOUCHDOWNS

1. Gale Sayers, 14 (1965)
   Walter Payton, 14 (1977)
   Walter Payton, 14 (1979)
2. Walter Payton, 13 (1976)
3. Rick Casares, 12 (1956)
   Neal Anderson, 12 (1988)

RECEIVING TOUCHDOWNS

1. Ken Kavanaugh, 13 (1947)
   Dick Gordon, 13 (1970)
2. Harlon Hill, 12 (1954)
   Mike Ditka, 12 (1961)
   Curtis Conway, 12 (1995)
   Brandon Marshall, 12 (2013)

PASSING YARDS

1. Erik Kramer, 3,838 (1995)
2. Jay Cutler, 3,812 (2014)
3. Jay Cutler, 3,666 (2009)
4. Jay Cutler, 3,659 (2015)
5. Jay Cutler, 3,274 (2010)

RUSHING YARDS

1. Walter Payton, 1,852 (1977)
2. Walter Payton, 1,684 (1984)
3. Walter Payton, 1,610 (1979)
4. Walter Payton, 1,551 (1985)
5. Walter Payton, 1,460 (1980)

PASS CATCHES

1. Brandon Marshall, 118 (2012)
2. Matt Forte, 102 (2014)
   Allen Robinson, 102 (2020)
3. Marty Booker, 100 (2001)
   Brandon Marshall, 100 (2013)

SACKS

1. Robert Quinn, 18.5 (2021)
2. Richard Dent, 17.5 (1984)
3. Richard Dent, 17.0 (1985)
4. Richard Dent, 12.5 (1987)
   Richard Dent, 12.5 (1993)
   Khalil Mack, 12.5 (2018)

GLOSSARY

defense: players who try to stop the other team from scoring

draft: to choose new players for a team

field goal: a score of three points in football made by kicking the ball over the crossbar

franchise: a team that is a member of a professional sports league

fumble: when a football player loses hold of the ball while handling or running with it

halfback: a football player whose main jobs are to block and run with the ball

Pro Bowl: the NFL's all-star game

rookie: a first-year player in a sport

roster: the list of players on a team

sack: when a quarterback is tackled for a loss of yards

turnover: losing the ball to the opposing team

wide receiver: a football player whose main job is to catch passes